HASTINGS
THEN & NOW

MARK HARVEY

The History Press

First published 2011

The History Press
The Mill, Brimscombe Port
Stroud, Gloucestershire, GL5 2QG
www.thehistorypress.co.uk

ISBN 978 0 7524 6208 0

Typesetting and origination by The History Press
Production managed by Jellyfish Print Solutions and manufactured in India

CONTENTS

ACKNOWLEDGEMENTS

With thanks to both my parents for their patience during the development of – and help with the finishing of – this book.

Hastings Reference Library and their very patient staff.

The numerous locals who have provided various pieces of information and useful leads.

INTRODUCTION

Hastings has changed dramatically since the town was a Roman port. Sadly, there is no longer any trace or clue as to where this was located. It was originally built in the natural valley between the East Hill and West Hill, upon which the town's castle resides. There are mentions of various attacks on English soil between 700 and 1100, when Kent, Sussex and Hastings all suffered. The Bayeux Tapestry is believed to show a house in Hastings being burnt to the ground, and possibly the construction of the castle.

During early medieval times, Hastings became an important part of the Cinque Ports confederation and housed both troops and ships for the king; it was also responsible for the protection of the coastline. During the twelfth and thirteenth centuries there were constant raids by the French, and this usually resulted in the town being set on fire. As part of its duties as a Cinque Port, the *Ann Bonaventure* of 70 tons was sent to help beat the Spanish Armada. During the dissolution of the monasteries in the sixteenth century, land and property that was meant to revert to the Crown was concealed by local landowners. This 'problem' was discovered at the end of the century and Hastings was given a charter under Elizabeth I so the lands in question could be leased. The town was given self-governing status in 1588, in a charter which is still active to this day. At the end of the sixteenth century, a new harbour was built for the town to help stop its decline. Alas, in one hour a great storm in this era destroyed all the work and left the residents near penniless.

During the next hundred or so years the town settled into its rôle as a poor fishing port, and the great Cinque Port became a distant memory. It was during the second half of the eighteenth century that Hastings began to be the town we recognise today. During 1771, Thomas Hovenden, the landlord of the Swan Inn, realised the potential of the town for bathing: the problem was that no suitable accommodation for guests existed. Through the efforts of the landlord, Hastings was recognised as a resort and soon more lodging houses began to appear – as well as bathing machines and a guidebook.

As Hastings began to grow over the next century it came to the attention of London architect James Burton, who decided it was the ideal location for his new town to be built. In 1828, the foundation stone of the St Leonards' Hotel (Royal Victoria) was laid, and St Leonards-on-Sea was founded. The following decades were busy, with new developments – and railway – arriving in the area. Views once dominated by farmland and grazing cattle were replaced with miles of roads, buildings and development. Before the beginning of the twentieth century, Hastings and St Leonards became one borough. During the early twentieth century, huge developments were made, with modern buildings and a new promenade attracting an increasing population. Although some parts have changed little, others have been transformed.

Mark Harvey, 2011

THE ALBERT MEMORIAL

THE PRINCE CONSORT, Albert, died on 14 December 1861. His memorial in Hastings was funded by a local group of subscribers. The stone obelisk, in a Gothic style mount, was designed by Edward A. Heffer of Liverpool, and in November 1862 the mayor, T. Ross Esq., laid the foundation stone. Although the tower was finished in a little over a year, the clock (by Thwaites and Reed of Clerkenwell) did not arrive until June 1864. The council were hopeful that the clock would be working on Saturday 11 June, striking hours and quarters. Within a year, however, there were complaints about the clock chiming at night; the council thereafter experimented with silent night-time running. Due to its location the clock suffered salt corrosion, and in October 1892 a Croydon firm was employed to replace dial components and glass on all four faces. Other work was carried out after a 1903 report

by the Borough Engineer noted rotten stonework and crumbling joints; part of the structure was rebuilt. The clock remained an essential part of town life until the 1970s, when the top of the tower was damaged by arson. The council had the pinnacles and belfry removed – supposedly for safety reasons – and in late 1973, citing the same reasons, the tower was demolished.

The area is still known locally as The Memorial, yet few people walking past today realise that this was also the site of a stream through the old America Ground. This area of the town is now mostly pedestrianised but was once the only way, by crossing a bridge, to pass through the front of the town. The original bridge was a wooden construction and was destroyed in a gale in 1800. It was replaced in stone, but the stream was culveted in 1836. The area has now changed in many ways, but it is still part of the centre of the town. This postcard view (left) was taken from the seafront end of Harold Place, looking towards Havelock Road. There was also a road crossing, which is now part of Queen's Road. The gardens and circular roof visible to the left of the picture are the underground public toilets, which opened on 12 December 1901. These were replaced later in the century with new, more modern facilities. The year 1978 saw the last film to be screened at the Orion cinema, located above WHSmith on Robertson Street. Many of the buildings in this area have survived both wars and continuing developments. Note: the postcard view was photographed before the existence of the promenade. On the right of the picture is a public house originally called the Denmark Arms; this building was destroyed by enemy action in the Second World War.

ALEXANDRA PARK

ALEXANDRA PARK LIES within a steep-sided valley or chine, largely wooded at its northern extreme. Archaeological evidence, including fragments of pottery and the existence of structures that may have been charcoal kilns, suggests the existence of an early Stone Age village here. By the end of the eighteenth century, Hastings was developing quickly as a notable South Coast resort. Early guidebooks from about the 1790s highlight Old Roar Gill as a particular point of interest: 'The situation was beautifully romantic; for after long heavy rains a large body of water tumbles over with a tremendous roar that is heard a mile off.'

In 1849 the Eversfield Waterworks Co. was formed to supply water to the town's growing population. They leased land from the Eversfield Estate, and by 1852 the Shornden and Harmers

Reservoirs had been built. Construction of the Buckshole reservoir had also started. At the other end of the park, construction of the Hastings to Ashford railway line had got underway, and the huge embankment formed became the southern boundary of the park. In May 1864 the council inspected the long awaited (and long delayed) St Andrew's Gardens, which they had taken over at the beginning of that year. Within a couple of years, the swans acquired for St Andrew's pleasure grounds were to have the companionship of a pair of foreign ducks, three moorhens and other aquatic birds, a gift from the Water Committee. A water fountain and an island for the birds were adopted.

St Andrew's was expanded by the donation of 9 acres by Mr Elphinstone in 1874. Over the next twenty years, facilities (including a refreshment tent) were added, and in 1867 the Gas Board Band was given permission to play in the gardens and a bandstand erected. In 1877, renowned landscape gardener Robert Marnock began one of his last works, introducing plants and shrubs to the park on a budget of £250. Marnock had designed the layout for Dunorlan Park, Tunbridge Wells, and Sheffield Botanical Gardens. The Prince and Princess of Wales (Princess Alexandra) officially opened the park on 26 June 1882, and the park, by now some 77 acres, was renamed in her honour. Gradually its area would increase to a little over 100 acres. The house at the park gates, Saxonhurst, was built by Joseph Catt in 1870. Two statues of Norman knights at one time stood in its garden. As the twentieth century dawned, a sum of £1,700 was made available for the building of three lodges within the park for wardens and custodians. During this period several handsome boats were made in the form of swans, to be part of a fleet for hire on the main pond. Over the years the park has seen many rallies and parties, all recorded by the local media. New improvements enhancing this beautiful area promise that the park will continue to develop to meet the needs and refresh the spirits of local residents and visitors.

ALL SAINTS' STREET

ALL SAINTS' STREET is one of the oldest streets in Hastings; here is only a brief look at its history. In about August 1848, the Courthouse Street extension was finished, linking the High Street with Old Saints. £455 was spent on buying properties and then clearing them away, particularly No. 86 All Saints' Street and three cottages in its garden. The town's old stocks had to be moved, as they were in the way; they were placed closer to the jail at the end of the original Courthouse Street. The stocks were finally removed in 1853. As this was a main thoroughfare, the street was 'macadamised' during August of 1850. In 1852 a Girls National School had opened in All Saints'. In August 1870 the council agreed to contribute £150 towards widening All Saints' Street.

The Ebenezer Chapel off Tackleway was improved during May 1873: old properties were cleared so that the chapel was now visible from All Saints' Street, and the building was extended

All Saints' Street, Hastings.

to Tackleway. The chapel's galleries were extended and widened, and lit by gas; seating was added for up to 350 worshippers. It reopened on 27 May. A large new drinking fountain at the top of High Street and All Saints' Street, set in a prominent wall connecting the two streets, was opened on 2 April 1879 by Mrs Shepherd, in memory of her late father, Francis William Staines, a resident in the borough for thirty-six years. The cost was nearly £1,000. The fountain has now gone because of the development of The Bourne. A Fishermen's Institute, at No. 97 All Saints' Street, opened on Tuesday, 19 December 1882; it was a new charity, offering fishermen an alcohol-free alternative venue for social events. In October 1905 a fire at Home Pub, No. 44 All Saints' Street, gained a strong hold and spread to the New Moon pub at No. 45, and to No. 43 All Saints' Street. Serious damage was done to the buildings by fire and water.

The most noted resident of the street was Cloudesley Shovell, who was born in Cockthorpe, Norfolk in 1650. Through family connections he joined the Royal Navy as a cabinboy in 1664, and his career progressed steadily over the years. On 22 October 1707, as Admiral and Commander in Chief of Queen Anne's Navy, he was aboard his flagship *Association* when, it was said, he ignored warnings about the weather and steered the whole fleet towards the rocks on the Scilly Isles. The *Association* foundered, and sank within four minutes. All 800 crew died that day. It was reported that when Shovell was washed ashore, he was still alive – he was murdered, or so the story goes, by a local woman, who stole the ring from his finger.

BOHEMIA ROAD

BOHEMIA ROAD BEGAN as a turnpike road. Part of the road was renamed Magdalen Road in September 1853, and at about the same time Linton Road was also created. During improvements in 1865, stone pedestrian crossings were placed across the street. In May 1865 work started: this was to include a pub on the corner of Tower Road. In August 1870 a tender from G. Bridgland saw work start on building St Paul's School, on the corner of what would become St Paul's Road, for the sum of £1,666. The architects were Jeffery & Skiller. On Saturday, 4 August 1883, Lady Brassey laid the foundation stone for the new St Peter's Church, at the top of Chapel Park Road, just before its junction with Bohemia Road. The contractor was John Howell, and building costs (excluding the site)

would be more than £10,000. It was paid for through the munificence of an unknown lady member of the congregation. The style was Early English, with red bricks specially made at Maidenhead, and the terminal stones were by Doulton; the nave was to be 90ft long, and the apex of the roof 78ft high.

At the beginning of 1894, the watch committee recommended that St Paul's Working Men's Club, on the corner of Bohemia Road and Salisbury Road, should be converted into a police and fire station. These were both located to the left of this picture, and a little further down the road. The project was costed at £1,300. This area also held a Temperance house, one of several around the borough, as well as a telegraph office. The improvements continued into the new century: the road was paved in traditional Hastings wood blocks from 1904; tram lines arrived a year later, causing severe disruption to the traffic. To the right, just out of shot, was the Bohemia picture house, and further down this road was the Bohemia Place Estate, built by order of Princess Sophia (daughter of George III), who resided there for a while. The 'Forty-Seven' Estate was eventually owned by the Briscoe family, who sold it to the Borough around 1966. Over the following ten years the site was redeveloped as a civic centre. The new fire station opened in February 1971, costing £193,000, and became Hastings Central Station. The Police Headquarters moved to purpose-built premises, costing £400,000, in July 1972, when the old building closed. Finally, during July 1975, the new Law Courts opened on the same site; the original house has since been demolished. Nothing can now be seen of the former gardens.

BULVERHYTHE ROAD

THE BEXHILL ROAD, on the other side of the bridge, was one of the original main routes into Hastings and is the location of one of the old Turnpike Taverns, the Bulverhythe, built in the days when there was still a marsh, salts and a port. The name means 'a landing place for people'. Messrs John Reeves and W.L. Vernon purchased 21.5 acres on Bulverhythe Salts during September 1883. The site adjoined the South Coast Railway, extending from the Coastguard Cottages to the Bull Inn at Bulverhythe. The land was part of the Papillon Estate and has since been found sufficient for the erection of nearly 500 houses.

Important developments on the Bexhill side of the railway line at Bulverhythe were occurring during March 1883, when building operations were being pushed forward. Bulverhythe Road had just been laid out, and the building plots marked. The Elworthys designed the semi-detached houses that were built at its western end by local builder Peter Jenkins. The narrow Bexhill Road was about to be widened, and the cliff adjacent to the road cut back, the Filsham Estate having granted some ground to the council for this purpose. The steepness at the bottom of Harley Shute was eventually levelled, and a good carriage road made all the way to the Corporation boundary. During 1905, a footbridge was constructed over the Haven to link the new Bulverhythe roads with Bexhill Road. This enabled people from the new estate to access the main thoroughfare more readily, and later to reach a new tram stop. The first section of the new tram line – from the Bo-Peep Hotel to Bexhill – opened to the public on Monday, 9 April 1906. The section of line had been completed in time for the Easter Holidays, and the Hastings and Bexhill tram services were based at the Bulverhythe Depot on Bexhill Road. In mid-1906 this line was extended again, to Cooden Beach.

The beaches here once witnessed the destruction of the second German submarine to be washed ashore in Britain during the Second World War. The boat, UD 131, which had broken free of a tug during a gale, was eventually broken up and sold for scrap. The area survived the Second World War with minimal damage. The last major development in this area took place during the 1950s-60s, when new railway sheds and workshops were erected.

BURTON ST LEONARDS' ARCHWAY, EAST LODGE

THE ARCHWAY WAS built in 1828 on Grand Parade to the east of Burton St Leonards, and marked the entrance to James Burton's premises. The arch was in the style of Chester Terrace entrance in London: eight Doric columns with an elliptical arch over the road, and flanked by two smaller arches. The north of these arches was designed for pedestrian traffic, whilst the south was constructed as a home for the town's beadle, the first being a man called Harman. This arch was later converted into a small shop.

However, this grand edifice narrowed the road and caused problems for traffic, especially with the expansion of the town. In November 1886 Hastings Council discussed the removal of the St Leonards' archway, which had marked one of the original entrances to the development of a new town, forming the eastern boundary of the original town of St Leonards. It stood across the seafront,

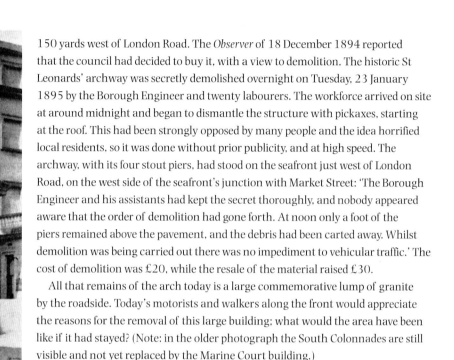

150 yards west of London Road. The *Observer* of 18 December 1894 reported that the council had decided to buy it, with a view to demolition. The historic St Leonards' archway was secretly demolished overnight on Tuesday, 23 January 1895 by the Borough Engineer and twenty labourers. The workforce arrived on site at around midnight and began to dismantle the structure with pickaxes, starting at the roof. This had been strongly opposed by many people and the idea horrified local residents, so it was done without prior publicity, and at high speed. The archway, with its four stout piers, had stood on the seafront just west of London Road, on the west side of the seafront's junction with Market Street: 'The Borough Engineer and his assistants had kept the secret thoroughly, and nobody appeared aware that the order of demolition had gone forth. At noon only a foot of the piers remained above the pavement, and the debris had been carted away. Whilst demolition was being carried out there was no impediment to vehicular traffic.' The cost of demolition was £20, while the resale of the material raised £30.

All that remains of the arch today is a large commemorative lump of granite by the roadside. Today's motorists and walkers along the front would appreciate the reasons for the removal of this large building; what would the area have been like if it had stayed? (Note: in the older photograph the South Colonnades are still visible and not yet replaced by the Marine Court building.)

BOROUGH CEMETERY

THE NEW 19-acre borough cemetery on the Ridge was consecrated by Dr Gilbert, Bishop of
Chichester, during November 1856. This followed several parish cemeteries being closed by the
1847 Act of Parliament. There had then been open disagreement in council circles about where
the new borough cemetery should be built, how much it would cost, who would get the contract
and who would make money out of it. When opened, the area had two chapels of remembrance,
a pair of lodges and a boundary wall, all built of sandstone on a brick foundation. Some of the
stone had come from council works across town. The first burial, on 2 December, was that of the
well-known local builder John (Yorky) Smith, who died on 23 November. Ironically, he had strongly
opposed the cemetery being on this site. During 1898, Hastings council agreed the expansion of
the cemetery by 7 acres and 3 rods. Before the end of the century, an area had been designated

for war graves, and this was used for both world wars. The respected architect Henry Carpenter died on Saturday, 13 November 1897 at his residence, No. 133 Marina. He first came to Hastings in 1850 and practised for many years in Robertson Street, designing many of the principal buildings erected around that time. He had also laid out the original cemetery. Over the next forty years there are numerous accounts of extra land being purchased for the extension of the official cemetery, bringing the space to over 73 acres. From the early 1900s, talk of crematoria was constant, and requests were made before the war to locate one here. With the outbreak of the First World War, the whole process was delayed. In 1938, Mr Holland W. Hobbiss, a local architect, designed and budgeted for the new crematorium to cost in the region of £12,000. Due to frugal times, the scheme was never undertaken: instead, one of the original chapels was to be used for the crematorium. The new crematorium at the cemetery was officially opened by the Earl of Verulam on 3 October 1955. The first cremation took place on 1 November, that of Alice C.C. Jones, an eighty-three-year old widow, of Blacklands Drive. The 1960s saw the last big improvement to the site, with a new Superintendent's house being built and other buildings converted into offices. At the end of the decade, a former nursery was turned into a garden of remembrance for the crematorium.

MOUNT PLEASANT & CALVERT ROAD

THE *NEWS* OF May 1866 reported on the building progress in the central part of the borough. Areas under discussion included Blacklands, Mount Pleasant, Quarry Road and the Great Brook Estate. At the council meeting of 2 March 1877, plans for eighty-nine houses on the Mount Pleasant Estate were passed. On 4 June, seventy-one lots of freehold building land on the estate were sold for about £4,000. The remaining portion of the Mount Pleasant Estate was sold off at the Castle Hotel on 15 July 1878. About seventy of the eighty-three plots were sites in St Mary's Road, and the rest in Quarry Road, Manor Road and Mount Pleasant Road. At around the same time St John's Road was renamed Calvert Road.

The Mount Pleasant School for Infants was opened in May 1881, and was followed, a few years later, by a second set of buildings for seniors; it was then charging a fee for schooling. On 16 July 1890, the memorial stones of the West Hill Wesleyan Chapel, on the corner of Mount Pleasant Road and Calvert Road, were laid. The Methodist Church, meanwhile, was formally opened on Sunday, 24 May 1891. The Hastings School Board opened its new Technical School at Mount Pleasant School on Sunday, 15 April 1894. Technical instruction was a requirement of recent legislation, and a plain but very substantial building had been erected for £3,000. Around 1878, the wooden bridge over the railway linking to St Mary's Road was replaced with a more substantial version. Towards the end of the nineteenth century, the Mount Pleasant Hospital was erected, also known as the Hastings Isolation Hospital. This had a mixed and varied life before being demolished in the 1970s.

Although tram lines were being laid to Mount Pleasant, there was a trial run of the new motorbus on 31 December 1904, to test its hill-climbing powers. It went up Old London Road with a full load, at 6mph, returning down Mount Pleasant Road to the Memorial, and then to Silverhill. It could carry thirty-four passengers, with a 20hp four-cylinder engine. The engine for a second bus was expected to arrive on 4 January. The coachwork of both vehicles had been built by Herbert Hunter, of 20 Waldegrave Street, Hastings, at his works in Mann Street. By 1905, with the tram line in use, there was a petition to the council for a new penny fare from Mount Pleasant to the Memorial.

The public house on the corner is the Mount Pleasant; however, there is also a 'Milkman's pub' listed in this area and it is not known whether they are one and the same establishment. The pub in question is believed to date from about 1891.

CAROLINE PLACE

CAROLINE PLACE ORIGINALLY fronted Castle Street, leading on to the seafront where the roundabout and car park are now located. At one point there was a shipyard (one of several on the seafront), which in May 1848 launched the new 10-ton pleasure yacht *British Lion* from Caroline Place. It was the largest public pleasure boat on the beach, built for Messrs Payne and Bumstead. Heavy seas on Monday, 11 April 1898 did much damage to boats near and on the beach. One craft was washed away entirely, and pieces of its wreckage were later discovered near the Lifeboat House. The Stades at Caroline Place and Denmark Place were torn to pieces, and gangs of men cleared tons of beach debris strewn along the thoroughfare. According to local archives, this was a regular occurrence.

The recommendation of the Stonebeach Committee in 1906 to erect a timber extension to the stone groyne of some 40ft, opposite the Royal Oak Hotel, Caroline Place, brought strong protests from the boatmen along the seafront. A petition, signed by most of the licensed boatmen, expressed concern at the danger of many small boats passing the extended groyne when the extension would only just be covered by the tide. Through the early years of the twentieth century many changes were made to the area, for both transport and local amenity reasons. During 1959 a new roundabout, with an illuminated fountain, and a block of flats were built at the junction of Castle Street and Pelham Parade. Together with other road improvements, this meant that Caroline Place was lost. The car park which covers the remains of Caroline Place was opened in July 1987 on the beach opposite Pelham Crescent. It cost £360,000, but there had been a delay in enacting the Act of Parliament that allowed the council to charge people for the use of the beach, so for the first few weeks parking was free. The Act also legalized the charging of fees to use Rock-a-Nore car park, which the council had been running illegally since the late 1940s.

Most of the buildings in this postcard view (left) have now been destroyed, by fire, bombing and demolition, to make way for road improvement. On the far right of the card is seen the very end of Pelham Parade. The road running along the front was just a narrow thoroughfare in the earlier image. There are numerous archive pictures of children playing here, and of public concerts using this area.

FRIENDLY SOCIETY

CAPLE LE FERNE was originally designed in 1897 by Jeffery & Skiller. The first occupants of the house were a Major and Mrs Tubbs. Although the Major died shortly after the turn of the century, Mrs Tubbs continued to live in the house for the rest of her life. During 1922, the premises were purchased by the London and General Omnibus Co. and opened in 1923 as a convalescent home for the company's members. Residents had to be either current employees or have retired from the London Public Transport industry. The provision of sickness insurance meant that when members were signed off long-term, and had been hospitalized, they were entitled to a period of convalescence at this home. On arrival most would have been amazed to find a large manor house with all the

modern amenities and facilities. The cost of conversion, £12,000, was paid entirely out of the Trust's own money, raised by members' subscriptions. The opening ceremony was conducted by the Assistant Managing Director of the London Traffic Committee, Mr H.E. Blain, OBE. Most London busmen did not personally own a vehicle, so the home had to be located near to good transport links. Nevertheless, a garage was provided.

The modernisation of the home was overseen by Mr Stanley J. May, architect of Southampton Street, London, who had adapted every conceivable item to the owners' wishes. The fully refurbished home was to include a library, a billiards room, a lofty dining-room with vaulted ceiling and stained glass windows, as well as a fine oak-panelled recreation room. It was all very different from most care homes of the period; thought had gone into both the decoration and furnishing of the property, and there were no whitewashed walls or hospital-type fittings. From both the upper floors and the viewing tower there were fine and uninterrupted vistas of both the town and surrounding countryside. During 1927, a large, eighty-six-bed extension was added to the property as the Trust had increased its membership – and thus the demand for the home. There are numerous postcards of this period showing that there were two to three beds per room, and the dining-room was set up like a large hotel.

In 1956 the home became the property of the Transport and General Workers' Union. During the transition, an additional building was acquired for both accommodation and recreation rooms. In 1993, due to a reorganization and asset clearance, a change of ownership saw the property become a residential language school for overseas students. A few years later, in 2001, the entire property sold for £1 million; it became an orphanage for children from overseas. In 2005 it became a rehabilitation centre. There are still many busmen who have fond memories of this property, and a painting of it has pride of place in the boardroom of the Transport Workers' Union.

HASTINGS CASTLE

THE CASTLE WAS begun during 1066 by William of Normandy. This was the second such building constructed by him, the first being Pevensey. The castle is believed to have been some form of wooden construction before it was rebuilt in stone. On Christmas Day, 1066, William was crowned king, and by 1070 had ordered that the castle be rebuilt. The castle was held by the Count of Eu during the Norman period. The castle was refortified in about 1220; during 1287, however, a great storm caused large parts of the cliff to collapse, taking chunks of the castle with it. This was also the end of Hastings' time as a Cinque Port, as silting had changed the harbour size. After this the castle was abandoned, and only the chapel of St Mary remained in use. During the Hundred Years' War, the town was regularly attacked by the French. Much damage was done, and many buildings burnt. This affected the castle, and dire weather caused further erosion, bringing more of the castle down. The end of the castle came in the sixteenth century, when Henry VIII dissolved the monasteries: everything of worth was taken from the castle. Land, lead, bells and any other valuables were seized and taken for the Crown. What remained was purchased by the Pelham family in 1591 and used as an area for farming, with the ruins being covered by vegetation and all but forgotten. During 1824, the remains were rediscovered and excavated, and several valuable and interesting finds were uncovered. The Pelham family remained the owners of Hastings Castle until 1951, and were thus able to remodel areas of the castle and grounds as needed. This resulted in the building of Pelham Crescent at the bottom of the cliffs, on the seafront. Building work started in 1824 and continued till 1828, and large amounts of the castle cliffs had to be removed to accommodate the grand design. As the cliffs were removed, the original castle chapel was lost – and this is how the church in the Parade below gained its name. The newly developed area then became an attraction for the Victorians, and started the revitalization of Hastings from a fishing port to a tourist attraction. (Victorian image courtesy of the Library of Congress, LC-DIG-ppmsc-08427)

EAST HILL LIFT

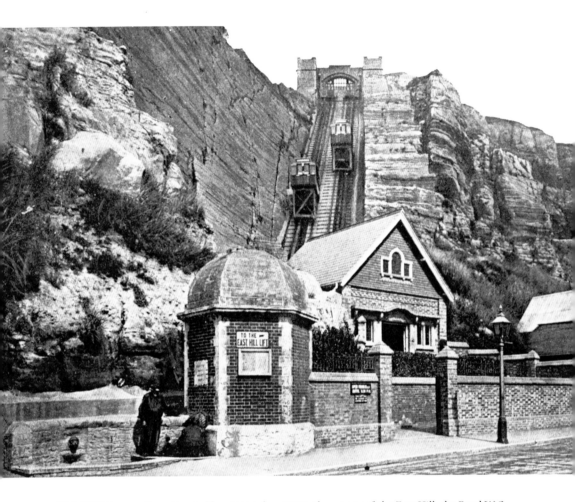

AT A TOWN council meeting held on 7 October 1892, the owner of the East Hill, the Revd W.C. Sayer-Milward, declined to sanction the proposal for a passenger lift. By 1900, however, an Act of Parliament allowed work on the lift to be commenced. It would run beside the steps up from Tackleway. The cars would hold twenty people and would take a minute and a half to run up or down. The total cost was estimated at £5,100. Some councillors doubted that it would pay for itself; others raised religious objections to Sunday openings, even though that would be its busiest day. In June 1902, after numerous construction difficulties, test runs began on the two carriages: 'An incident which showed the absolute safety of the East Hill Lift occurred yesterday Friday 18 July 1902 morning, whilst a trial trip was being made... about 15 yards from the top, the car jumped the rails. The safety apparatus caused the car to stand still, however, and the occupants walked to the bottom. It is satisfactory to state that the defect is by no means serious, and will soon be remedied.' Following this accident, the *Mail* of 26 July reported that the lift opening had been delayed.

The borough engineer refused to take possession for the Corporation until the car wheels had been replaced by those with larger flanges.

The East Hill Lift was finally opened in 1903 by Hastings Borough Council, and apart from a few minor accidents and problems it has run smoothly ever since. It is one of the few remaining funicular railways to have survived in Britain. Until 1973, the system operated on a water-balance system, both stations containing water tanks and pumping equipment. After 1973 the station was modernised with new carriages to provide for the future. The line runs at a gradient of 78 per cent for 267ft on a 5ft gauge double track. The lift was powered in its early years by the nearby dust destructor. This was built in 1888 as a waste-refuse incinerator (the first in the country) and provided excess steam which, until the demise of the plant in 1933, was used for a multitude of purposes, including pumping water for the East Hill's counter-balance mechanism. The lift was closed for over a year in 2009 for full refurbishment and reopened in 2010. It should survive another 100 years without any problems.

The refuse/dust destructor, opened in 1890, is to the right of the view in this postcard (left). Apart from producing power for the East Hill Lift and other installations, it served as a stone-crushing plant and a fish-meal processing facility, and heated seawater was also pumped into the town for various uses. This area has changed considerably, and the remaining prominent features are the lift and the fishermen's huts.

HASTINGS STATION

THE FIRST RAILWAY to Hastings was approved in 1839. It was to run along the coast from the west as far as St Leonards, to the newly constructed Hastings and St Leonards stop (later West Marina). This eventually opened in 1846. It was an extension to the London, Brighton & South Coast Railways (LBSCR) line to Lewes. During 1851, the Bo-Peep tunnel was created, and the line extended through Gensing Park Station (Warrior Square) to Hastings Station. A second line was completed in the area in 1851, this time by competing railway company South Eastern Railways (SER), which reached as far as Hastings and came in from Ashford in the east. Shortly after, the SER were responsible for the construction of the two tunnels from Hastings to link up with the existing LBSCR line at St Leonards West and its own existing line through Battle to London. Services officially started in February 1851, but the two rival companies fell out, resulting in several blockades and many arguments. This resulted in an unsatisfactory service between Hastings and St Leonards. The various feuds meant that the original station had to become triangular shaped, to allow separate platforms and ticket offices for the two competing companies.

During 1858, Prince Albert passed through Hastings en route to Prussia. He was met by an enthusiastic crowd at Hastings Station. In October 1879, work began on both enlarging and improving Hastings Station. About fifty workers had arrived in the town for the creation of St Andrews' Arch. During 1899, the SER and LCDR companies merged to become the South East and Chatham Railways (SECR). This was eventually to form the Southern Railway (SR) in 1923 and incorporated both old companies, as well as the London & South Western Railway. In December 1901, a dramatic collision at Hastings Station occurred. On the 28th, an SER train ran into a loaded truck, knocking it off the line and derailing the engine.

The disputes between the rail companies were finally settled in the early twentieth century by the courts. The construction of a new, Neo-Gothic style station with one large central booking hall was begun in 1931. This was possibly the work of (or influenced by) Edwin Maxwell Fry, who built many stations during the period. It was designed to provide four platform faces arranged in the form of two islands. Goods facilities at the rebuilt site were spacious, but when the 1935 electrification scheme came around, there was no room to accommodate EMU stabling facilities – neither was it preferable to have empty stock taking up much needed platform capacity. The solution was to extend the third rail beyond Hastings, to Ore, where a substantial area existed in between the 'up' platform and goods sidings for a large EMU maintenance shed. This in turn has now been replaced with a modern structure, and sadly the old building has been lost.

This picture (left)is from the 1880s, and shows the original tringular-shaped station for the separate train companies, and the beginning of the goods area. This station was to be demolished in 1930, and has since been replaced twice.

GAIETY THEATRE

WHERE THIS CINEMA now stands was originally the location of Castle Mews, a small development of residential properties. The Gaiety Theatre opened on 1 August 1882 and was designed by the noted theatre architect Charles John Phipps, in association with the local architectural firm Cross and Wells. The first performance was of Gilbert and Sullivan's English opera HMS *Pinafore* by Mr D'Oyley Carte's company. Until then, Hastings had lacked a good theatre, but this compared favourably with any of the provincial houses in the kingdom. There were eight boxes, orchestra stalls, pit stalls, pit, dress circle, upper circle, amphitheatre and gallery, and the auditorium seated 1,600 people. The building was 71ft long on Queen's Road and 118ft long on Albert Road. In October 1883, the celebrated writer Oscar Wilde lectured at the Gaiety Theatre, to the title 'The House Beautiful', and there was a very fair attendance: 'He dealt with the practical side of asceticism and gave some useful advice on house decoration and furnishing.'

In 1888 the company running the theatre became public, and in about 1896 the theatre participated in an experiment with the new-fangled telephone. In August 1904, the famous actress Ellen Terry started a week's performances at the Gaiety Theatre. She played Portia in *The Merchant of Venice*. It was reported as having been quite a long time since there was such a fashionable gathering in the Gaiety. Since the beginning of the twentieth century there have been at least two fires reported in the building, but neither did substantial damage. On 14 May 1932 the Gaiety Theatre closed to live shows with a production of *The Desert Song*.

The Gaiety was then converted into a cinema and the auditorium was completely altered, losing 500 seats in the process. It was managed by the local Randolph Richards' circuit and reopened on 12 December 1932 with Conrad Veidt in *Rome Express* and Laurel and Hardy in *The Music Box*. In 1966, the Richards' circuit was sold to the Classic Cinemas chain and the Gaiety Picture Theatre was renamed Classic Cinema from 1967. In May 1971, it was converted into a twin-screen cinema: screen one, in the former circle and front stalls, had 767 seats; and screen two, in the rear stalls, had 165 seats. It then passed to the Cannon Group and was renamed Cannon, with the addition of a third screen in 1984. It then became MGM for a short while. A management takeover gave it the ABC name in June 1996, and in around 2001, it was taken over by Odeon Theatres. It now has four screens, whose seating capacities are 129, 176, 151 and 127. The original picture postcard (left), from about 1900, shows many differences to the structure. Most notable are the changes to the ground floor and the original entrance, which has moved to the corner. The detailed balustrades to the roof have also been removed. This is the last of Hastings' cinemas, the only one to survive into the twentieth-first century.

GEORGE STREET

GEORGE STREET IS one of the oldest roads in Hastings and was originally the main thoroughfare of the town. In 1838, No. 42 George Street was built to be the home of the Hastings Literary Institution and a print works. The new George Street Market opened on 7 August 1833. Built by Hastings Corporation next to the Anchor pub, it was intended to be the town's fish market, replacing the open-air one on the beach, but fisherfolk opposed the idea. Three fishmongers were incarcerated in the Courthouse Street gaol on 6 September 1833 for continuing to use the beach. The first long-living Hastings newspaper was published in May 1848. The *Hastings and St Leonards News*, based at No. 42 George Street, cost 3 pence. It was published initially by William Ransom Jnr, but that August he became ill and his father, William Ransom Snr, took over.

Excavations for drains in George Street during 1857 revealed the remains of former fortifications, and a copper Henry VIII groat was found nearby. The Hastings Old Bank in George Street closed in June 1857 due to bankruptcy. It was the town's oldest bank, formed by local entrepreneurs in 1791. The worst gale since November 1881 hit the town on the night of 23/24 October 1882. Many buildings around the town suffered damage, and West Street and parts of George Street were flooded. The spray was higher than the tops of the houses in George Street. The artist Dante Gabriel Rossetti is known to have stayed in this area between the 1860s and the 1880s. He was to marry in St Clement Church, where a memorial to him is still in place. There are numerous letters and drawings attributed to him in the town. There was a serious fire at No. 8 George Street, in 1883, at the premises of Mr Austin, the gunmaker. The fire was difficult to put out, being in a basement, but fortunately this was achieved before the gunpowder and fireworks exploded. The Local Government Board carried out a public inquiry on 21 September 1899 into the laying of modern drains, water and electricity for George Street and its surrounds. There were major floods and damage in the early twentieth century due to a massive storm, which resulted in changes to the defences and to local buildings.

There have been many businesses here over the last 150 years, but the most prominent and the longest lived was Butler's Famed Emporium, which opened in 1888, the founder being a local councillor. In 1976 a huge fire destroyed the T.W. Barnes scrap shop adjacent to the Emporium. This was just down the street from the postcard view (left), and is now an open space called Butler's Yard. The Emporium was sold by the grandson of the original owner in February 1986, and is now closed. Just a year later this narrow street was pedestrianised and was reopened by the actor Bernard Bresslaw on 25 April 1986. The street is now a busy and vibrant mix of drinking establishments and independent shops.

HASTINGS COLLEGE / GRAMMAR SCHOOL

THE COLLEGE CAN trace its origins back to 1619, to the will of the Revd William Parker, rector of All Saints'. A few days before he died, the vicar set out the foundation charter of the institution which was to become Hastings Grammar School. It was another twenty years before the first schoolmaster was appointed, but the charitable foundation that still supports the college today can be traced back to the reverend's gift. In May 1880, Hastings Grammar School opened in temporary premises at Bleak House, Stonefield Road.

The new Grammar School, in Nelson Road, was opened by the Mayor of Hastings on 4 July 1883. There was considerable controversy: it was aimed at middle-class children, but the building had been paid for by the Magdalen Charity, which had been set up to benefit the poor. One of the more famous pupils of the school was Archie Delaney (or Grey Owl). Readers may have seen his film biography, *Grey Owl,* starring Piers Brosnan. Grey Owl is commemorated at Firehills and was rumoured to have used school facilities to make his gunpowder. In 1933 Hastings Scout group was formed and used the school gymnasium as their meeting place and scout hut. In September 1964 the Grammar School moved from Nelson Road to new premises in Parkstone Road, and in 1978 it was renamed the William Parker Comprehensive, after its 1619 benefactor. Sadly, in April 1972, the former Grammar School in Nelson Road was demolished, having stood empty since the William Parker Comprehensive had come into official existence, a merger of Hastings Grammar School and Priory Road Secondary School. The Priory Road buildings continued in use. The High School for Girls was renamed Helenswood.

GROSVENOR CRESCENT

IN MARCH 1893, the western parts of Hastings were improved by the pretty ornamental gardens at West Marina (Grosvenor Gardens) and two railway stations, and the local paper felt that 'the neighbouring estate owners ought to do their utmost to serve the public interest by pushing forward building operations.' The Eversfield Estate still had in hand the building spaces under the cliff facing Grosvenor Gardens, 'a choice site for the erection of a series of good residences', and architectural drawings had already been made for Nos 1-24 Grosvenor Crescent. The crescent of houses was to follow the course of the River Asten, which can no longer be seen as it has been culverted. Elworthys had designed the semi-detached houses that were now being put up at its western end by local builder Peter Jenkins. Bexhill Road was to be widened, eventually leading to a wide and broad road to Bexhill and beyond, the Filsham Estate having granted some ground to the council for this purpose. The steep Harley Shute was to be levelled, and a good carriage road made all the way to the Corporation boundary.

Also in this area was a temporary structure, the iron church St Saviours, measuring 30ft by 60ft, which had been erected in memory of Mr G.H. Lake. In December 1897 the council agreed that the new row of houses being erected by the park should be called Grosvenor Crescent. This was also the area where the first Hastings tramway death occurred, in April 1922: Miss Annie Eliza of No. 22 Salisbury Road, a domestic servant, jumped from the moving tram and fell, striking her head on the stone curbing. Today the gardens are by a busy road but still provide excellent recreation facilities. The Bo-Peep public house (at the end of the terrace on the right) is a well-known landmark on the way into Hastings along the now developed Bulverhythe Road. It is not in its original location or style. This is the second Bo-Peep Hotel and pub. The original building, a more ramshackle affair, was named the New England and had stood where the West Marina station was erected. This was to change with the construction of a Martello tower during the Napoleonic Wars. The pub became the Bo-Peep, earning a good reputation. It also gave its name to one of the two rail tunnels to Hastings. The money for the new pub came from the compensation of the rail company, and for a brief time it was called the Terminus Inn. It was very popular with the navvies and related workers, both for the railways and development locally. Until at least the early twentieth century there were many complaints, both of smuggling and of other inappropriate activities at this location, before it became a respectable boarding and lodging house. Today it is still a hotel and pub.

HASTINGS PIER

THE FIRST PILE of Hastings Pier was driven at 3 a.m. on a December day in 1869, after a year of debate. It was to due to open on August Bank Holiday 1872. The first cargo of iron works for the pier had already arrived at Whitstable harbour. For more than a week at the beginning of 1870, the heavy screw piles had been hauled to the Parade at White Rock to be stacked ready for use. A large iron pile for the new pierhead hit a hard object and broke the large screw in July 1871. The object was a large oak trunk, 3ft wide, 24ft long and weighing about 2 tons. The pierhead was evidently in the very heart of the ancient forest. The new saloon, when completed, would be the biggest room in the borough.

The nearly finished Hastings Pier was visited for the first time in May 1872 by the crew of Thomas Brassey's large yacht *Eothen*. The pier was opened for public inspection on the same day, and was officially opened on a Bank Holiday, 5 August 1872, by Earl Granville, Lord Warden of the Cinque Ports, with the Mayor, Thomas Ross, Mr Kay-Shuttleworth MP, and Thomas Brassey MP. There was heavy rain. The coastguard formed a guard of honour at the station, the Artillery and Rifle Volunteers lined the pier, and there was a salute by the town's guns at the pier head. During the Bank Holiday of 6 August 1883, only eleven years after opening, 94,000 people had passed through the turnstyles. With the pleasure steamer *Nelson* plying from the pier every weekday, the council agreed, in August 1885, to create a new landing stage for craft, at a cost of £1,140. The enlarged landing stage on Hastings Pier was opened for steamboat traffic on Thursday, 1 May 1890.

The first landing stage was along the east side of the promenade, beside the pavilion, but the work of the last ten months had extended this to the end of the pier and then taken in the whole of the pierhead. The staging now ran round both the east and south side of the Pavilion, but not the west, because that was too exposed. The staging was in three levels. About 400-500 tons of greenheart woods had been used, plus 130-140 tons of iron. As many as four steamers could use the pier together. At the end of January 1899, the pavilion closed for refurbishment. Barely a year later the pier suffered its first fire, during a concert, in June 1900. Although flames were seen from the White Rock, the fire was soon extinguished. In March 1907, a nightwatchman failed to notice a burglary on the pier, which left a scene of devastation. During the early years of the twentieth century, smaller buildings were erected on the pier to house various entertainments. The council acquired the front of the pier in 1913 to provide an extension and additional shops, but four years later, on 15 July 1917, fire destroyed the pavilion; the flames could be seen across Hastings. Following the rebuild, in 1926 a Shoreward Pavilion in Art Deco style was added. Over the years, the pier has played host to all kinds of events, often to concerts and dancing. Some of the façades have changed and new buildings have appeared. The landing stage fell out of favour after the war and, in common with other resorts, a decline in business signalled changing fortunes. Sadly, the pier recently suffered another great fire, but with luck, and with the recent award of a National Lottery grant, it will rise from the ashes to become something new and exciting for residents and tourists.

KINGS ROAD

GENSING STATION ROAD was developed between 1840 and 1860; this is the road ending at Gensing Park Station. Both of these were named after Gensing Farm, for whose land the development was proposed, and both were renamed in 1882 to become Warrior Square Station and Kings Road. (There had been some confusion with the other Gensing Road in town.) The road was mostly built in what old guidebooks described as 'the Venice style'. This appears to be

fairly unique to the area, and indeed to the country as a whole. Sadly, there is no information currently available on when and by whom the buildings were built and designed. At the beginning of January 1868, a site for the proposed British Schools was purchased for £700 within the triangle where Gensing Station Road meets London Road. There were to be three schoolrooms, and Alfred Vidler's tender of £2,224 was accepted for building the premises, which were to open in 1868.

There have been many businesses located on Gensing Station Road/Kings Road, more than enough to fill a book of their own. Two of exceptional interest include a post office, opened on 27 April 1879, and the Wilson & Son Baker's (which has now closed). There was also a Woolworth's, but its opening is not recorded. The road was the main shopping street for the St Leonards' area, and in 1901 the council spent £2,000 to pave the surface. During its time the road has seen many processions and pageants. Kings Road had a fire depot, Frowd Chass Dairy and Gensing Hall Stores for all provisions. Another notable shop in the area was one of the oldest barber's in the town, Pierce and Holes, whose business, established in 1898, was continuous until its closure in 1980. Today the road is still the central shopping area and new development continues to make changes.

LONDON ROAD / BARLEY ROAD JUNCTION

THE ROAD TO the left in the postcard is Old London Road, leading to the village of Ore, running up behind the market cross. The road to the right is now Harold Road but was previously Barley Lane. Between 1880 and 1890, improvements were made to Barley Lane and a new road was created to serve the Clive Vale Estate. The foot of Barley Lane was merged into the newly formed road, and the stables in front of Breeds Place were demolished to extend the road onto All Saints' Street. At the time of this postcard, The Bourne as a road did not exist, and access to the seafront was via either the High Street or All Saints' Street. The building to the left survived and now bears a plaque for Titus Oates, one of the instigators of the Popish Plot. He was in Hastings in about 1674, serving as a curate, and was later imprisoned in Hastings. The railings have now gone, replaced by a new road following the bed of the River Bourne. There are map and reference notes of several houses behind the railings, called Ravenshurst, Hastings Cottage and The Wilderness. By mid-1950, however, the site is marked as empty scrub, and it is believed that the properties were destroyed in the Second World War by a single bomb.

The tramway companies, introduced in 1905, used the Market Cross as a turning point. The Cross is believed to have been replaced in 1901 with a new version to commemorate the accession to the throne of Edward VII. The Old Town tram system was never electrified, and so passengers would transfer to horse-drawn buses to continue into Hastings. Between 1900 and 1905, improvements to the Old Town reduced poverty and squalor. Bourne Street, which ran only to the courthouse, was relaid, and several slum properties were demolished. Around twenty years later it was decided to extend The Bourne along the old river course to Old London Road. This plan was delayed until about 1958, as the war put all road proposals on hold. The first section of The Bourne, from the seafront to the newly built Roebuck Street, was finished by early 1959. Work started on the second section, north from Roebuck Street, in mid-1962 and was finished about a year later. The new road followed what had been a footpath alongside the River Bourne, which is now piped. By 1963, all the work had been completed. It had caused much controversy at the time as there were other routes proposed for the road that would not have divided the Old Town into separate areas.

To the left of this picture (left) is The Stables, one of the finest example of domestic Georgian architecture. John Collier, five times mayor, converted four cottages into the current building, which now houses a theatre, well reputed as a member of the Little Theatre Guild for over fifty years. To the right, behind the trees, is the magnificent All Saints' Church, also called Upper Church, a Grade I listed building dating from 1436. One of the noted curates of the church was Samuel Oates, father of the aforementioned Titus. The church has several interesting features, including a rare Father Wills Organ from 1878, and is in virtually unchanged condition; above the chancery arch (and rediscovered in 1876) is a painting of the Judgment called 'The Doom'. This was once the very edge of the township of Hastings.

LONDON ROAD

THE SCHOONER *FAIRY*, 110 tons, broke her back on the groyne at the unloading slipway at the bottom of London Road on a January night in 1869, during a south-west storm. Captain Eastland, who had half shares in her, lost everything, as there was no insurance for vessels beached to unload.

The turnpike road system came to an end on Sunday, 1 November 1875, and their absence was greatly appreciated. During 1860 a new drinking fountain was placed at the bottom of the road 'for the working classes.' This was possibly in memory of Richard Beagley. The new Christ Church in St Leonards, on the corner of Silchester Road, was consecrated on Thursday, 20 November 1884. The Marina and seafront were served by new roads. On Sunday, 25 June 1894, the foundation stone

was laid for the tower and spire of Christ Church. The tower was to be 190ft tall, making the church the largest edifice in the town. It would cost £3,500 and was to be finished by the end of the year, when the bells were installed. The spire and tower were formally dedicated on 5 February 1895, and a special service of celebration was held.

Between the late 1880s and 1905, both electricity and the trams arrived in London Road. A letter in the *Mail* complained in June 1905 that the shelter at the bottom of London Road was occupied by 'labouring class loungers, smoking and lying around, sometimes with their feet up on the benches.' Between 1890 and 1900, Robert Tressell, author of *The Ragged Trousered Philanthropist*, lived in this road. In May 1929, the council experimented with traffic lights at the London Road/Norman Road Junction. This was to result in the installation of several permanent sets of lights in key locations around the town. The Regal cinema in London Road, opposite Pevensey Road, had been closed for many years and was demolished during May 1973. In 1977, Gundolphus house was built on this road, the tallest building in Hastings (replacing the Regal cinema which had previously been on the site).

MARINE COURT

WHERE MARINE COURT now stands was originally part of James Burton's St Leonards. The South Colonnades (numbers 22 to 32, built in the 1830s-40s) were demolished to make way for this landmark building. At the time there was little concern for building conservation, and although some protest is recorded it was largely ignored. The foundation stone was laid on 30 November 1936 by Robert Holland-Martin, Chairman of Southern Railway, for what was then the Sun Lounge, a

striking post-modernist building from a period when 'concrete and bold' was the keynote for the future. The design imitated the lines of the Cunard ship *Queen Mary*, which had first sailed on 30 November 1934. The architects were Kenneth Dalgleish and Roger K. Pullen. When it opened in 1938, with 153 flats, three restaurants and a ballroom, the Court was 170ft high and was described as the highest dwelling place in Britain. The structure is fourteen storeys high, and from east to west 416ft in length. When viewed from the east or west Marine Court is very tall and slender, and from the beach, south or north, the full expanse of the building dwarfs all others on the seafront.

Marine Court was of a pioneering steel-frame construction, like the earlier De La Warr Pavilion in Bexhill-on-Sea. All the apartments have southerly, sea-facing balconies to recline on and spacious modern living interiors. There were also walkways to the promenade and seafront, accessible without having to leave the building or cross the road. (These were permanently sealed during the early 1940s due to the threat of invasion.) A competition was held to name the building and despite some derogatory suggestions Marine Court was chosen. At the eastern end, the curved lower floors protrude like a ship's bow and the floors above recede like the stacked decks of an ocean liner. At the west end the balconies end in a graceful curl, leaving a gap at the stern. Damaged at its eastern end by bombing during the Second World War, restoration of the building took place in 1949-1950. This is one of those rare buildings that have to be seen from a distance to appreciate its scale and splendour; sadly spoiled by modern 'improvements' like double glazing, the building is currently being restored to somewhere closer to its original splendour. Apart from a similar design in New Guinea, this building is unique and shows the grace and design of Modernist pre-war architecture.

NORTH LODGE

NORTH LODGE, ONE of the original gateways to the town of St Leonards, spans the Upper Maze Hill (named after the early maze in the private gardens which were adopted for the public in the 1880s). Originally built as a tollgate at the northern entrance to St Leonards by James Burton in 1830, in a mock Gothic castellated style, the Lodge guarded a toll road which ran from here and joined the main London to Hastings road. Before it was built there was no development around this area, and most of the land was farmed. On the wall above the main arch of North Lodge is the shield and anchor emblem which was often used on Burton buildings. The Burtons incorporated it into their family arms in 1902. Improvements were later made with the Sedlescombe Road development. North Lodge became the family home of Miss Helen Wood, James Burton's

ARCHWAY PAY GATE
AZE HILL ST LEONARDS ON SEA.

grandaughter, who died at the house on 19 January 1903, the last of three sisters. A later resident was author Henry Rider Haggard, author of *King Solomon's Mines* and *She*, who lived there from 1918 to 1923. Along the road beyond the archway is a splendid late Victorian property, which was once home to St Augustine nuns and later became a nursing home. The property is now the main building of a local hospice. The house has become apartments, and is protected by the Burton St Leonards' Society. The archway was damaged by a large vehicle in 2002 and following its repair has remained closed to vehicles.

NORMAN ROAD

NORMAN ROAD BEGINS at what was Lavatoria Square (Mercatoria), where the washerwomen lived and worked. This area was also home to the Horse & Groom pub, built in 1829 for the Burton labour force. The pub has a horseshoe-shaped bar and interior. In 1841, the wall between Lavatoria and Norman Road was demolished, opening the area up. It was developed further with the building of Warrior Square's new properties and a railway station. In 1861, Hastings Council approved the buying of land for a new police station, on the corner of Norman Road and Mercatoria, and on 19 September, the *News* reported that the council had accepted a tender for £598 from Mr Bridgland for building the station. A meeting was held on 8 December 1866 to promote a new public hall in St Leonards, the rooms to include hot and cold baths, Turkish baths, a dining-room, a reading-room, and a meeting-room for 1,300 people. The building was to be adjacent to London

Road and Norman Road West. The new Norman Road Wesleyan Church was dedicated on 5 June 1901. It had been built for £4,521 by Mr W.G. Morgan; the architect was Mr James Weir of London, and total costs were about £5,500. The new church was larger than the old square one, burnt down in 1900, which had been built about 1837. Adjoining houses had been pulled down to make room for it. It was in Gothic style, with a steeple 90ft high, and backed onto Shepherd Street, where it had a schoolroom. The Norman Hotel in Norman Road was put to auction in July 1909. The bidding stopped at £3,000 and it went to James Wright, the tenant in occupation.

In May 1929, the council experimented with traffic lights at the London Road/Norman Road junction. As a result, several sets of permanent lights were installed in key locations around the town from October 1934. In November 1913, the first purpose-built cinema in Hastings opened in Norman Road, to be called the Kinema Palace, seating 650. During August 1952 the Kinema was enlarged and renamed the Curzon. It closed in 1977 after offering *Raid on Entebbe* as its final show. Several of the properties in the original postcard (left) have now gone, mostly due to war damage.

HOLLINGTON CHURCH

ALSO KNOWN AS 'the church in the wood', this building started as St Rumbold Church/Chapel and was located near to a mansion and small scattered hamlet. Since its founding in the middle of the thirteenth century, the building has been in isolation, surrounded by the woods. Although it is not mentioned in the Domesday Book, a will of the Count of Eu from 1139 states that a place of worship existed on this site. The chapel was replaced by a church in the mid-thirteenth century, with the first recorded vicar, in 1288, one John de Levenynton. The first dedication to the church came in 1562 and was to St Rumbold, though over the next 150 years the name St Leonards began to be applied to the building.

The church, despite its isolation, has continued to serve its parish, but it had declined into a poor structural state by about 1834. Sir Charles Montolieu Lamb of Beauport Park wanted the church demolished and moved nearer to his residence, but the building was saved by parishioners who objected to the move. Work was started on repairing the church in 1847 and would continue for about twenty years. The church had to close in 1861 whilst the works were ongoing. Matilda Dampier paid for all of the works in lasting memory of her mother. After the work, the only medieval parts left were the west and north walls, some of the tower and an ancient bell. During 1897, Hollington became part of the Borough of Hastings, and since that time little work has been done on the building. A lychgate was added in 1937, and general repairs were commissioned in 1964. This was the last remaining private burial ground in the town, and the earliest gravestones are from 1678. Like all areas of the country, the borough of Hollington grew over the first half of the twentieth century, mainly driven by the building of council houses in the vicinity. Although it has lost its rural setting, the woodland around the church has been protected as one of Hastings' ancient woodlands. Most of the structure is of bluestone and Caen stone; both the roof and the cap on the tower are tile hung. There are several stained glass Victorian windows, in differing styles. Some of the windows may be by the firm of Clayton and Bell. The location of the church in the wood is explained by a story involving a battle between the Devil and the builders. Every night the work carried out the previous day would be destroyed, and the materials taken away. A voice spoke to the builders, claiming that the site belonged to the Devil and demanding the church be built elsewhere. The church was successfully rebuilt on a new site to the Devil's liking, and a wood grew around it to conceal it.

OLD FISH MARKET AREA

THE NEW GEORGE Street Market, built by Hastings Corporation next to the Anchor pub, opened in August 1833. October 1884 saw the ceremony of laying the corner stone of the major new sea-defences to be built at Rock-a-Nore, following serious damage to the Old Town in October 1884 (which could have been avoided if the council had built defences such as this in time). The council had refused to do so, hoping that the fishing boats would have been forced to move to

Rye, thereby opening up the Stade to development. Public protest had forced the council to change its attitude and obtain £20,000 for this project. The designer was Sir John Coode, marine engineer. The new fish market opened in March of 1956 amongst the net shops. Its predecessor, demolished in early 1956, stood where today's amusements are located on the seafront. The Fishermen's Museum, in Rock-a-Nore Road, was declared open on 17 May 1956. The area has changed considerably since then, with road and car park improvements. Towards the end of this area was the dust-destructor, built in 1888 and in service until 1933; as well as powering the East Hill lift, it pumped heated seawater through the mains for both the swimming pool and bathing facilities, and other private facilities that were connected. On the Stade area, a rock-crushing plant, fish-meal processing and a facility to treat contaminated laundry water were also built. Some of the buildings on the left remain, but the paved area on which the cart rests is now part of the new road development, built from the 1920s onwards.

CHRIST CHURCH, ORE

CHRIST CHURCH, ORE, was built in 1858. It was designed by Alexander Gough, and a Holman Hunt painting is replicated in one of the windows. There is a fine pulpit in oak with a carved font, and a fine brass handrail. The communion rail is in oak with simple moulding, on wrought iron supports with gold leaf ornamentation. The official consecration of the church took place in September 1870, the service led by a local bishop. In July 1882, Trustees of the Hastings and Flimwell Turnpike erected a new toll bar near Christ Church, Ore. Much of what is now opposite the church was only just being planned.

The church in Ore had its own Associated Lads Brigade, presumably to fight in or support the British Army. In a 1905 article it is noted that a Lieutenant H.C. Duke, an officer of the Christ Church Ore Lads Brigade, was leaving his mother country for Canada. Ore at the time had several workhouses and slum areas; it is interesting to note that the vicar in 1905 was also appointed to be the workhouse chaplain. In 1897, when the borough of Hastings was being extended, Ore village became part of Hastings and St Leonards. The beginning of the twentieth century saw the area as an impoverished and destitute manor. With the arrival of trams from the beginning of the twentieth century, workers in the area were able to travel on a cheap fare to building and work sites around town. Much of the area around the church was rebuilt between 1900 and the 1920s.

After sustained controversy between residents and planners, the sea-front area to the right has become the site of the Jerwood Gallery.

QUEEN'S ROAD/PRIORY FIELD

DURING 1851 THE Queen's Road area of Hastings became famous for the first airborne escape of a convict: the Duke of Brunswick used a balloon to evade capture and sail to France. Queen's Road started to come to prominence in Hastings between 1860 and 1875, when plots of land were made available for purchase. The lower Queen's Road area (or America Ground) was at one time marshland with a stream running through it. During the winter of 1859/60, the Priory Stream was culveted, the Priory Bridge removed and the marshes drained. A pedestal with three lamps was put up on the site of the bridge, and a new road laid from York Buildings to White Rock.

A letter of October 1861 suggested a cricket ground be built on Priory land. A public meeting was held at the Havelock Hotel Assembly Room on Wednesday 9 March about using the Priory Meadow as a 'Central Cricket and Recreation Ground'. A committee was formed, which wrote to the two women who owned the ground, the Countess of Waldegrave and the Viscountess

Holmesdale, asking for a lease of the land. The *News* of 25 March reported that the meeting reconvened on Wednesday 23 March at the same place, with a large and enthusiastic attendance, including many prominent people. George Scrivens, who had played a large part in finding a cricket ground, was appointed chairman. He reported that both their ladyships had acceded to the request. The meeting decided that two acres were to be levelled, turfed and drained, and fencing erected around the site, at a cost of about £500. The ditch running through the meadow would be filled in, with a pipe in lieu. It was generally believed that the ground there was above sea level, and therefore safe. The committee was to take possession on 25 March and would do their best to have the ground ready by August. The existing cricket ground on the East Hill had been improved but was difficult to access. A subscription list was to be started to raise the funds, and £130 9s was contributed as the meeting ended. The ground would be used for cricket, circuses, booths, flower shows and similar entertainments.

In July 1864, the New Priory Meadow opened with a match between committee and subscribers and thus the East Hill Ground was replaced. Although the land for the new ground was initially leased in August 1872, it was eventually bought for £5,000 on the promise that it remained a place of recreation. The first Australian cricket team to come to England played at Hastings in June 1868; a team of Aborigines. The Aborigines scored 119 + 185, Hastings 152 + 113 for 4. Afterwards there was a boomerang display, and Dick-a-Dick defended himself against fifty or sixty hard-thrown cricket balls with a stick (he was not hit).

The Town Hall, in Gothic Style, was designed by Hastings architect Henry Ward in 1880. Most of the rest of the buildings within this area are post-1880, with later alterations by the council, some due to bomb damage. In May 1984, when the proposal for a new shopping centre was discussed, it was decided that the drainage of the land and the transport infrastructure would be inadequate to support the building. However, this decision was revoked in 1986; the centre has permanently changed both this view (left) and that from many other places within the town.

PELHAM CRESCENT

THE PELHAM FAMILY were the owners of Hastings Castle from 1591-1951 and remodelled parts of the castle and grounds as needed. The building of the Crescent opened up more of the town for future development. The Earl of Chichester decided, in 1824, that Pelham Crescent and St Mary in the Castle were to be built, and they were designed by the architect Joseph Kaye. Building started in 1824 and continued until 1828.

A large section of the castle cliffs had to be removed to accommodate the grand design. In fact, once started, the removal of the cliffs was extended along the seafront to allow for further projects. The extensive cliff cutting and subsequent building works were carried out by John Smith, considered in his day one of the greatest builders of the early nineteenth century. He came to Hastings in 1815 and built most of Wellington Square, parts of St Leonards for Burton, Pelham Crescent, the Arcade and St Mary's Chapel; Pelham Crescent's Georgian splendour and St Mary in the Castle Church were considered his major works, the church being named after the chapel in the castle. In a now demolished section of Pelham Crescent, Charles Dickens stayed at the Marine Hotel

during his 1861 tour. Of the noted residents of the Crescent, Barbara Leigh-Smith Bodichon, one of the founders of the women's rights movement in England, leased a property for its sea views, and the photographer William John Willmett established his Fancy Repository at No. 14 Pelham Crescent, being listed as its proprietor in the trade directories of 1911-1915 and as 'W.J. Willmett, Photographer' in 1918.

In the post-war years, people moved away from town-centre living and both the church and the Crescent started to fall into disrepair. In 1951 they were awarded a Grade II listing for the quality of their architecture, but despite this the church was deemed surplus to requirements in 1970, its final service being held on 13 September of that year. Queen Elizabeth, the Queen Mother, supported the council's efforts to acquire the church in the 1980s after it had become derelict. After lengthy discussions, major renovation work was undertaken to save the structure and build a new arts centre. Today Pelham Crescent is virtually unchanged and remains one of the chief architectural glories of the town. St Mary in the Castle has become an art gallery and auditorium. Most of the Crescent is now listed and has been fully restored.

PRIORY ROAD

THE PRIORY ROAD area had several prominent and commercial wind- and steam-driven mills – there were at least five windmills, several on the site now occupied by the new school. One archive noted a large steam mill there, built by Mr Ward of Ore Parish in 1849 and demolished in 1874. The mills were cleared from 1850 onwards for road improvements and to make parcels of land available for sale. On 30 April 1873, an auction sold 126 plots of building land for £3,400. They were situated between Mount Pleasant Road and Priory Road. In 1873, there were no roads or houses in the large triangle formed by Mount Pleasant Road on the north, Priory Road to the south-east and St Mary's Terrace to the south-west. The Hastings Cottage Improvement Society built three large houses in Priory Road during April 1874. The Board decided that a new school should be built on the corner of Croft Road. The site would cost £1,100, and the new school would replace The Bourne Walk Schools, which were too small. It opened on Friday, 18 September 1891.

Local benefactor Mrs Mendham died on 21 May 1893 at her home in Uplands,
St Leonards. She had been very charitable, making provision for the construction of
Emmanuel Church in Priory Road, the vicarage, and the vicar's stipend. The church
opened in 1874 and cost £7,000. Mrs Mendham later paid £650 to enlarge the
church. By 1900 most of the building plots had been sold and served with roads, and
apart from some repairs after the war, most of the properties were built during this
time. There are records of numerous local businessmen and photographers living in
this road at the time of building. The Emmanuel Church, shown in the postcard (left),
has a memorial stone laid and donated in 1873 by Mrs Mendham, sister of the Revd
W.T. Turner of Ore, on the corner of Priory Road and Plynlimmon Road. John Howell
was the builder of the church, Jeffery & Skiller the architects. It was consecrated on
22 September 1874. By the 1890s the church was considered too small and closed
for enlargement; it reopened on 17 November 1892 to serve what was, at the time, a
very large and rather needy parish. This road was also home to the Fortunes of War
public house and stopping post, badly built in 1810 and then rebuilt thirty years later.
The pub survived the Second World War, despite heavy surrounding damage, but was
finally demolished in 1970 for road improvements. Priory Road is one of the few roads
in Hastings that have shown little change over the years – apart from the increased
number of cars, as one resident says.

QUEEN'S HOTEL

THE PROMINENT QUEEN'S Hotel on Hastings seafront was built in 1862 on part of the site of the America Ground. Originally, there were two cupolas on the roof of the eastern side, but these no longer grace the building. The hotel had a large forecourt, gardens and a slipway to the front, but this was much reduced to make way for seafront widening. In June 1882 the new Hastings Lifeboat was launched from the hotel slipway by Miss Kittie Arkoll, with the help of Sir Thomas Brassey. This was followed by a banquet. In 1869 the hotel was extended to provide larger beer cellars, an improved restaurant and a terrace for customers. In November 1894 the Queen's Hotel had re-opened after spending £8-9,000 on renovating the whole interior. It had been redecorated and re-furnished, and electric light had been installed. The exterior had been altered little, except for adding some balconies. In its early days the hotel paid dividends of 21 per cent to its shareholders.

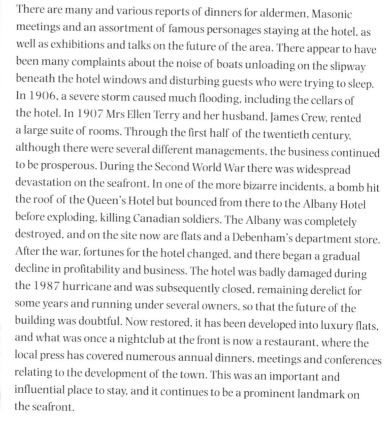

There are many and various reports of dinners for aldermen, Masonic meetings and an assortment of famous personages staying at the hotel, as well as exhibitions and talks on the future of the area. There appear to have been many complaints about the noise of boats unloading on the slipway beneath the hotel windows and disturbing guests who were trying to sleep. In 1906, a severe storm caused much flooding, including the cellars of the hotel. In 1907 Mrs Ellen Terry and her husband, James Crew, rented a large suite of rooms. Through the first half of the twentieth century, although there were several different managements, the business continued to be prosperous. During the Second World War there was widespread devastation on the seafront. In one of the more bizarre incidents, a bomb hit the roof of the Queen's Hotel but bounced from there to the Albany Hotel before exploding, killing Canadian soldiers. The Albany was completely destroyed, and on the site now are flats and a Debenham's department store. After the war, fortunes for the hotel changed, and there began a gradual decline in profitability and business. The hotel was badly damaged during the 1987 hurricane and was subsequently closed, remaining derelict for some years and running under several owners, so that the future of the building was doubtful. Now restored, it has been developed into luxury flats, and what was once a nightclub at the front is now a restaurant, where the local press has covered numerous annual dinners, meetings and conferences relating to the development of the town. This was an important and influential place to stay, and it continues to be a prominent landmark on the seafront.

PALACE HOTEL

ON WHAT WAS the site of the old White Rock brewery until 1886, and the Seaside and Pier Hotel
thereafter, an ambitious new hotel was to be built, at the foot of St Michael's Cliff. The Palace was
opened in December 1886 and was considered to be the best hotel in town, visible from Eastbourne,
and very soon depicted in tourist advertising. It had a frontage of 125ft. When the 80ft foundations
were being dug, human bones were found from the graveyard of St Michael's Church. The
structure was built by local men John and William Taylor, who were also involved in other building
projects around the town. Unfortunately, in May 1893, the builders were declared bankrupt after
a bad property and development deal at The Swan in Hastings Old Town. The exterior of the Palace

featured richly decorated gables and dormers; the interior of the hotel was luxurious. Apart from the main entrance there was a side entrance for servants. On the fifth floor of the tower a third entrance was built for working-class patrons to access the upper floors and to allow access to the kitchens. There were 140 apartments arranged through the building. Most of these rooms offered luxury en-suite accommodation, and some had several interconnected areas. The tower had one bathroom per floor, and was aimed at working-class tenants and servants. There was extensive modern piping for the building, with cisterns housed both in the building and in a large water storage facility in the cliff to the rear.

The whole complex was served by two passenger and luggage lifts, three dinner lifts and a wine lift, all operated by hydraulics. One of the lifts rose through the tower, and all were encased in open wirework-style bronzed ironwork. The whole building was illuminated by both incandescent electric and gas lighting. Much of the interior was in polished teak and walnut, with furniture to match. The hotel boasted two separate coffee salons and a restaurant, a gentlemen's smoking-room and a ladies' room. The extensive basements held the engine rooms, wine cellars, boot rooms, general storage and staff accommodation.

In September 1900, Charles Harcourt Wordsworth was killed by a sink strainer falling from one of the hotel windows. Another tragic accident happened four years later in December 1904, when a young waiter fell to his death down the baggage liftshaft. Reports in one section of the press claimed that a painter had fallen from the hotel as a result of his using the wrong type of knot to secure himself to the building. Luckily, the report went on, although he was killed, he missed a ladyship walking below. A footnote said it would have been terrible for a commoner to have hit one of the gentry. The hotel was used in both of the wars to billet troops: the first saw both the Royal Flying Corps and infantry, while the second saw RAF and senior officers. Today the hotel is converted into flats, with a pub below. The building's unusual prominence is the result of its extended tower at one side of the structure.

SEAFRONT GRAND PARADE

THESE IMAGES LOOK along the Grand Parade. Although there have been many changes here since 1800 – including the removal of a bluff headland, the construction of new roads and widening of the seafront – towards the end of 1890 most of the seashore still extended almost to the houses. Through traffic had to access relatively small roads into and around the shopping areas, and hotels were complemented with jetties and breakwaters as necessary (for their own use and in some cases for deliveries to the town). Grand Parade was originally named in 1853 when the sea wall and promenade walks were created. During the 1860s, the Marine Sea Wall project was commenced, and this is featured in the older photograph. The road along this stretch featured many hotels and lodging houses for holiday visitors.

The road at this point was only about 50ft wide, with an equal width of pavement. Major improvements came to the seafront from July 1926, when Sydney Little was appointed Hastings Borough Council Engineer and Water Engineer to implement a large-scale redevelopment plan.

This was to regenerate the town he described as 'like some beauty queen in decrepitude'. He became known as the Concrete King for the many important and innovative schemes he initiated, and was probably the single most influential Hastings planner and architect up to the Second World War. The council adopted Sydney Little's Front Line Improvement Scheme. Beginning in December 1929, he reclaimed land from the sea in order to redesign the seafront between Marine Parade and White Rock: there was no through road past the Queen's Hotel prior to this. The £111,300 project included the world's first underground car park, 846ft long and 60ft wide, backed by sunken gardens in Robertson Terrace. There was a new raised sea wall to protect against flooding. The first stage of the work was completed in 1931. During 1934, Bottle Alley was opened, linking White Rock to Warrior Square in a double-tier walkway. Originally the lower level had glass windows to protect from the elements. Hastings Council agreed Sydney Little's plan to rebuild the promenade and sea wall from London Road to the Bathing Pool, to be commenced in 1934, and the work was completed by December 1938. The underground car park was opened by Transport Minister Hoare-Belisha on 15 June 1936. Walking on the very long, straight promenade past numerous concrete Art Deco shelters, few people realise the height and extent of the space beneath their feet. It houses not only underground parking but also facilities for the sailing clubs and, at one point, public toilets and café facilities. Knowing the full extent of the construction, you begin to realise how far-sighted Sydney Little was: he was the father of modern Hastings. He not only created a visionary modern structure, but he also protected the top of it against increasingly high tides.

SILVERHILL JUNCTION

SILVERHILL IS NAMED after the eighteenth-century farm that once stood there. Silverhill Junction is where the A21 to London crosses the main road to Battle. This area was at one point home to poor families and housed the Rainbow Hotel Baths, which were seldom used. The postcard below looks down London Road from the junction toward the coast. There have been both police and fire stations in the area, but these were closed as a policy of centralization was introduced. During 1884, the Hastings Conservative Club opened on the junction just behind where this picture was taken.

The foundation stone of the church of St Matthew, London Road, Silverhill, was laid in September 1860, and the porch and tower were added in 1874. The newer, much larger St Matthew's was built in 1885, adjacent to the original church. However, there were insufficient funds to build a tower and spire. The old church was replaced by a modern hall in 1959 (which,

" The Old " and " The New " at Silverhill.

before that, had been used as the parish room). St Luke's Church opened in 1857 as an independent church, but soon became known as the Silverhill Chapel. Due to Sunday school overcrowding, a larger hall was added. Much of the surrounding housing stock is of Victorian origin and there are some fine and unusual architectural features. Hastings Council decided to split Sedlescombe Road into Sedlescombe Road South and Sedlescombe Road North in February 1903. This coincided with the arrival of trams in the area. The main tram depot was at Silverhill and is now the bus depot. Apart from the shops which crowd this area, there were also a garage/workshops and a council school on the corner of Paynton Road. Major improvements were carried out on Sedlescombe Road North during 1929-1930, including road widening. On 27 November 1952 the new 700-seat Silverhill Roxy Picture House opened on the corner of London Road and Beaufort Road. Elva Engineering built a racing-car factory in Sedlescombe Road North in 1959, which was opposite Ashdown House. Towards the end of the 1950s, and into the 1960s, the Ponswood Estate was developed. This changed the area and brought both more employment and more traffic. The town's last windmill, Draper's Mill at Silverhill, was demolished in June 1966 because of its poor condition. It had been built in 1866 and last used in 1941. During building works in and around this area many fossil remains have been found, including some almost complete skeletons. Today the area is a combination of shops and houses, with a new Asda supermarket being built on former works and housing land.

ST ANDREW'S ARCH / BRIDGE

JUNE 1846 SAW the commencement of a tunnel, to be known as St Andrew's Archway, starting at what was then Stonefield Road and Ore Lane. This was to enable more of the town to be developed and to provide access to what would be Alexandra Park. Within a couple of years, and certainly by 1849, cracks had already begun to appear in the structure, due to the embankment above. This was further aggravated by the opening of the railway line in February 1851. In 1877, Alderman John Howell drew attention to the serious need to improve the structure. The tunnel was narrow

and dark, and it allowed only one goods carriage to pass through at a time, causing consternation to the locals using it. An appeal to townspeople to bear some of the costs did not bear fruit. Toward the end of the 1890s it was decided that a new ornamental arch, which would cost £9,735, was to be built, and after discussion it was agreed that the railway company would contribute one-sixth of the costs and would not disfigure the new structure with advertisements. Eventually, a motion to construct a bridge/viaduct was passed by fourteen votes to five. Alderman Tuppenny was the main promoter of this replacement. The width of the tunnel had been only 19ft 6ins, but the new structure created a road nearly 50ft wide. Originally the western footpath was designed to pass on the inside of the pillars as they stand now, on the eastern carriageway.

During August 1897, whilst work was underway, a railways inspector fell down a deep shaft adjacent to the arch and died. On Friday afternoon, 4 November, a section of the roof at the northern end of the tunnel fell in. Traffic was stopped and buses to Spa and Mount Pleasant were suspended. Demolition of the structure began on the night of Saturday, 5 November 1898. It took three days, and the demolition spoil was deposited on the railway embankment. The new bridge, which had been erected above the tunnel, although not fully completed, was opened to pedestrians and vehicles to pass underneath on Tuesday, 8 November 1898. The bridge has served well over the years, and on 14 September 1976 the viaduct was Grade II listed.

ST HELEN'S PARK ROAD

THE *NEWS* OF January 1873 carried an advertisement for St Andrew's Spa, by H. King: 'An elegant Spa Room has been erected from the designs of H. Carpenter Esq, with a fountain in the centre, into which the water flows direct from the spring, without losing any of its purity and efficacy.' Admission was *2d* or *2s 6d* per month. It was on what is now the north-east corner of St Helen's Road and St Helen's Park Road. Gas lighting arrived around 1890. Buffalo Bill's Wild West Show on the 20 August 1903 drew thousands to Buckshole Field, St Helen's Road. Colonel W.F. Cody introduced a grand review, his 'Congress of Rough Riders of the World' and 'the U.S. Artillery'. A prairie emigrant train drove in and was attacked by Indians. Colonel Cody performed 'unrivalled feats of shooting from horses' and Johnnie Baker, the celebrated young American marksman, demonstrated his ability as a splendid shot: 'Never before has anything of such magnitude and

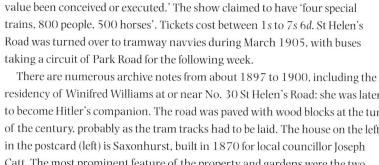

value been conceived or executed.' The show claimed to have 'four special trains, 800 people, 500 horses'. Tickets cost between 1s to 7s 6d. St Helen's Road was turned over to tramway navvies during March 1905, with buses taking a circuit of Park Road for the following week.

There are numerous archive notes from about 1897 to 1900, including the residency of Winifred Williams at or near No. 30 St Helen's Road: she was later to become Hitler's companion. The road was paved with wood blocks at the turn of the century, probably as the tram tracks had to be laid. The house on the left in the postcard (left) is Saxonhurst, built in 1870 for local councillor Joseph Catt. The most prominent feature of the property and gardens were the two large statues of Norman knights, or Saxon warriors. The councillor was highly respected in Hastings and oversaw the creation and development of Queen's Road. There was a light on the corner of the road to provide both a beacon for locals and travellers and a landmark. Miss Dorothy Catt was principal and founder of the Orchard School for Girls, which opened in 1929. The novelist Catherine Cookson lived in this area for a number of years after buying a house in St Helen's Park Road in 1954. During the 1970s, local improvements saw a large area of garden adopted by the council to provide bus-stop facilities.

ST LEONARDS GARDENS

JAMES BURTON WORKED with Nash on Regents Park, London, and St Leonards Gardens show that this influenced his planning of the layout here. He carefully noted the strong Neo-Classical style of Nash's Terraces with its mix of public buildings. The whole of the new St Leonards was built in a park setting with the wooded slopes and falls of water used to great effect. In the centre of his scheme was a space known as the Subscription Gardens. It was originally laid out as a private garden, with two separate ponds and a maze for both the Burton family and paying patrons, but the gardens were unfortunately little known or frequented, partly due to the scenery surrounding the development and the distraction of the sea nearby. In 1879, Hastings Council bought the Subscription Gardens seafront for £9,000, and they were formally reopened as the St Leonards Gardens on 17 April 1880, admission free, and greatly improved. The gardens proved very popular and gave Maze Hill its name. Gothic-style buildings are visible around the wooded valley.

The gateway to St Leonards Gardens is an imposing Burton building called South Lodge, which is actually two dwellings: South Lodge West and South Lodge East. This is a double villa with the central span forming the entrance to the park. William Ford Burton is known to have stayed in the South Lodge on many occasions whilst visiting St Leonards. The clock tower is a dominant three-storey tower in ecclesiastical Gothic style, and the clock was supplied by King George III's clockmaker to be the official timepiece of the area in its early days. The original buildings surrounding the park are Allegria, home of James Burton until his death in 1831. Towards the top of the park is the castellated villa now known as Gloucester Lodge, renamed after a visit by Princess Sophia Matilda of Gloucester.

During the 1920s and '30s there was a care home here for the blind, called St Dunstan's. Residents used the gardens for exercise, and there are still remains of the original braille signs placed in the gardens for their use. The home was built in the 1870s and was the residence of the Revd J.W. Tottenham. It was purchased in 1914 by the Dickens Fellowship as a Servicemen's Convalescent Home and then sold to St Dunstan's in 1920. Some of the original buildings have gone, but there still remains a large selection of mostly Regency and early Victorian houses. As you leave the Gardens through the bottom entrance you will see the old Assembly Rooms, now a Masonic lodge. The council recently applied for a Heritage Lottery Grant for the restoration of this garden, and work has now begun, another positive step for this historic part of St Leonards.

ST LEONARDS' PIER

THE SUCCESS OF Hastings Pier in the 1870s and 1880s prompted the construction of its rival in St Leonards. Several attempts were made, in different locations, to build a pier along the coast of the town. As Hastings unified as a town, construction work increased. Finally, a company was formed in April 1886 to build a pier at St Leonards. It would be 900ft long and was costed at nearly £20,000. The *News* of 29 April 1887 reported that a meeting had been held to discuss it. The ceremony of screwing the first pile into the beach for the new St Leonards' Pier, 50 yards west of the Royal Victoria Hotel, was performed by the Mayoress on Thursday, 1 March 1888. The engineer was local resident Mr R.S. George Moore. The pier finally cost £30,000 and was built by Messrs Head Wrightson & Co., of Stockton-on-Tees, using 1,500 tons of iron. The mayoress, Mrs Stubbs, wife of the Councillor Stubbs, screwed in the last bolt of the 22,500 in the ironwork substructure of St Leonards' Pier on Thursday ,9 October 1890. Several hundred people watched the ceremony, including the company chairman, Mr R.J. Reed. The St Leonards' Pier was deliberately 50ft longer than the Hastings Pier. Finally, in October 1891, Lady Brassey formally opened the pier.

One of its main features was a 700-seat semi-Moorish pavilion near its shoreward end, designed by Mr S. Humphreys. The pier's west toll house was destroyed by a severe gale in February 1896, as was as a large section of the landing stage. In 1904 the pavilion was turned into a fashionable lounge called the Kursaal. The St Leonards' Winter Orchestra played its inaugural performance at the Kursaal in November 1904, but further concerts were not a financial success, and they were ended on 12 February 1905. In May 1907, £50 was stolen from the pier. On 1 April 1909, an 'American Syndicate' took possession of it and carried out big improvements. The whole pier was painted and decorated, and six ornamental kiosks erected, each accommodating three shops. It reopened on 23 May 1901 as the American Palace. By August of that year a new pavilion had been built at the end as a roller-skating rink. This had two entrances, and the pavilion occupied the whole of the large round space at the top of the pier, painted in delicate colours of cream, blue and gold, and lit by gas (with further decorative illumination by electricity). Although the pier was visually attractive, it was a financial failure. Hastings Council was offered the pier for a mere £9,000 in 1927, and in 1940, because of the war, a section of the pier was removed as a defence measure, as happened with its Hastings rival. In October of that year, St Leonards' Pier suffered damage from a bomb attack, leaving it semi-derelict. It was hit by severe gales early in February 1943 and then seriously damaged by a major fire on 7 March 1944, described by the local press as a 'spectacular blaze'. In late December 1950 Hastings Council decided to purchase the pier for demolition. The Territorial Army carried out the final stages of removing the piles in the summer of 1953. Today there is no visible reminder of this pier, apart from a small plaque on the railings by a public car park.

WHITE ROCK

Hastings. Parade & S.

THE WHITE ROCK, Hastings, named in 1881, was previously Stratford Place and Precursor Place. Originally there was a bluff in this area that hindered the view down the promenade. The bluff was removed by the Victorians, since when there have been many changes to the site; Dorset Place was once known as Hollow Way, as it cut through the rocky outcrop.

Items for the Crystal Palace Exhibition were shown at Messrs Rock & Sons' carriage showroom at White Rock on 26-27 February 1851. The company took children of the Hastings Union Workhouse to the Crystal Palace by train on 31 July. Improvements planned at Rock's Carriage Works included a new Gothic building by John Kowell (architects Jeffery & Skiller). It was to be a great architectural feature of the development, with a bold archway 22ft wide and 20ft high. The *News* of 2 May 1873 reported that the new showrooms opened on Easter Monday. The previous year's trade had doubled.

During 1905, Fred and Thomas Judge began moving their growing business to Camera House at No. 42 White Rock. An indoor rifle range was opened at White Rock Villa by the Mayor in August 1909. The houses along this stretch are a mix of styles, built as the town expanded in the late nineteenth and early twentieth century. The White Rock area saw a new road and facilities for both bathing and recreation constructed around the turn of the century.

The annual meeting of the Hastings and East Sussex Hospital was held at the hospital in White Rock, on Tuesday, 14 February 1905. A large expenditure and reduced subscription meant that it was now over £1,000 in the red. On 19 August 1905, the governors of Hastings Hospital met to consider an offer for their present site. There was a strong feeling in favour of moving, and arguments were put forward for a new site. The £20,000 offer from Mr Arthur Hobart was supported and the matter was practically settled. Several years earlier the idea of moving had been opposed because it was felt that someone was trying to benefit from the wave of hotel building. The current hospital building, however, was too small, and a much bigger site at Horntye Field was considered. Towards the end of 1905, the council agreed in outline the proposal by Arthur Hobart for the acquisition of the Brisco Estate for the site of a 'Winter Garden'. On 2 September the Hastings Hospital governors decided almost unanimously to dispose of the White Rock site of the hospital to the same Mr Hobart. This paved the way for the White Rock Theatre and a new road behind it, with access from the seafront. The chosen designers were Charles Cowles Voysey and Morgan Hugh Townsend, and the theatre was owned and managed by Hastings Council. The theatre had several rather quirky features echoing local history, the most notable being the original seating capacity of 1,066. The opening performance was in April 1927, and it has since hosted an eclectic mix of opera, ballet and musicals. The open upper balcony, which was designed for fresh air and to view and listen to the pier bandstand performances, was enclosed in the 1970s to create a new coffee shop.

emorial.

ROYAL VICTORIA HOTEL

WORK STARTED ON building the new town of St Leonards during 1828, the creation of London architect James Burton. From 1828-30, he rebuilt the seafront. The first stone of the new St Leonards' Hotel, later to be the Royal Victoria Hotel, was laid on 1 March 1828, and it was opened in 1835 by the Duchess of Kent and her daughter, Princess Victoria. The original main door was at the rear of the building, as at this point the beach and promenade were only a few feet away. The hotel had been designed and built to attract a wealthy clientele. April 1849 saw the start of a three-month stay by Louis Phillipe, ex-king of France. He was in exile after escaping from the 1848 French Revolution in a fishing boat. The Queen of Belgium arrived on 29 June, remaining until the 20th of the next month (presumably to visit to the former king). Other royal guests included the

Duke and Duchess of Saxe-Coburg and Gotha, who were staying at the hotel during June 1850. The king of the Belgians visited in July 1858 to see the ex-queen of the French. Eight years later, the Prince and Princess of Wales were staying at the Royal Victoria Hotel. At about this time, it is rumoured, Mr Gladstone also stayed at the hotel, followed only four years later by the Crown Prince of Prussia and family in October 1868. Albert Victor and George Frederick, sons of the Prince of Wales, stayed at the Royal Victoria from 11 July 1873 for seabathing, visits, and drives, leaving on the 22nd. The Royal Victoria reopened on 19 November 1891 after renovation and alterations to the hotel, which had taken several months.

Twelve years later, major refurbishment was carried out, and the hotel reopened on 8 March 1904 after undergoing almost complete rebuilding, including the construction of a new main entrance to the front of the building and an almost entirely new frontage. The work cost in excess of £10,000 and took almost a year to complete. In the previous decade it had been acquired by the Royal Victoria Hotel Co. It had the latest labour-saving devices and appliances, and a billiards room with two full-size tables on the left of the main entrance. There was accommodation for nearly 200 visitors. The refurbishing work was carried out by Councillor John Parker of Clive Vale (who went bankrupt as a result). The promenade outside the hotel was widened in the 1880s to provide better access along the seafront, and it was to be redeveloped again in the 1930s with the creation of the long, straight promenade Hastings has today. The wood-block paving of the Marina outside the hotel was commenced in 1902, and tram lines arrived a few years later. The Royal Victoria buildings opposite the hotel were used as baths, and were demolished for road improvements.

WARRIOR SQUARE

WARRIOR SQUARE BEGAN as a proposal for a private subscription garden, and work started on it in 1852. The Square is home to many fine buildings and hotels. From August of 1852, Warrior Square Gardens hosted a band concert three times a week. Whilst Mr John Howell's workmen were building the west side of Warrior Square in 1855, numerous Roman coins were found. The Royal Concert Hall in Warrior Gardens opened on 13 October 1879. Originally called the Warrior Square Opera House, it was for many years the leading centre of entertainment and social functions in St Leonards. Many famous artistes appeared there, and it was the venue for large meetings, circuses, balls, banquets, speeches and exhibitions. Speakers were to include Winston Churchill, Captain Scott, Sir John Herschel and Horatio Bottomley. After the First World War the opera house was given a new lease of life, becoming an Elite Picture Theatre. It suffered bomb damage in 1940 and 1942, and was then used as an Admiralty store for the rest of the war. On the day the Elite was due to reopen after the war, Monday 23 June 1947, it was burnt down by a mysterious fire – one of the biggest and most spectacular in the history of the town – which destroyed most of the building.

The new Presbyterian Church of England on the north-west corner of Warrior Square and Terrace Road was opened on Wednesday, 14 March 1883. It cost £8,160. A meeting was held to form a new company that intended to create a gentlemen's club for the borough. It was agreed in May 1883 that £15,000 capital would be raised to purchase the large building comprising Nos 1 and 3 Warrior Square, on the south-west corner on the seafront. The Warrior House Hotel was built and opened at some time in the 1850s, 'a luxury hotel with many fine bedrooms'. The Grand Duke and Duchess Michael of Russia stayed at Warrior House in 1862. During the 1880s and 1890s, both electricity and gas were supplied at the hotel for the comfort of guests. Elizabeth Jane Stephens, sister of the proprietor of the Warrior Gate Hotel, was suffocated by gas while asleep in her bedroom in February 1904. It leaked from a pipe which had been badly repaired. The hotel closed in March 1983, and after standing empty for a number of years it was converted into luxury apartments with a restaurant below. The Borough was planning to acquire a site at the lower Warrior Square Gardens for a statute of Queen Victoria in September 1902. On 12 November, it was unveiled for an hour to allow an inspection by the committee. A few years later, in 1907, a new bandstand was erected. The gardens were purchased by the council in 1920 and the upper rose gardens were donated in 1930. War took a heavy toll on the area, as can be seen from numerous more recent buildings. Major restoration and landscaping work was carried out in 2001, the gardens being restored as a pleasant place to while away an afternoon.

GENSING PARK / WARRIOR SQUARE STATION

GENSING PARK STATION (Warrior Square) was created when the Bo-Peep Tunnel and Hastings Tunnel were completed in 1851. The station was constructed and owned by SER (South East Railways). Their rivals LBSCR (London, Brighton and South Coast Railway) had to pass through the station without stopping, until a court ruling of 1870. The Gensing railway station was to be improved in 1861, as there were no platform canopies, and travellers ran the risk of a drenching. By February 1862 most of the down-side improvements had been completed. Alterations started on the station in March 1865 after the terminus had been described as 'cribbed, cabined and

confined' during heavy summer traffic. Horses and carriages would no longer be forwarded from Gensing Station as of May 1868, but only from Hastings, where the platforms were longer, and because the delay in coupling on and off, trains was proving a hindrance to traffic on the line.

The improvements that had been promised through the 1860s were at last being carried out at Gensing Station in July 1869. The platforms were extended and a footbridge was built over the line. From December 1870, all passenger trains of LB and SC railways would stop at the SE Railway's Gensing Station, so it was now possible to book from there to any LB or SCR station, although the two companies kept separate booking offices until the 1930s. During December 1884, the plan for a new railway station, to be called Warrior Square, was approved by the council. This entailed rebuilding part of the booking office and remodelling the front approach. Very little has changed since then. A Hastings contingent of Volunteer Riflemen departed for the Front via Chichester during February 1901. Sixty of them marched to Warrior Square Station, where they were addressed by the Mayor before departure. This is the only station now available to the people of St Leonards, following the demolition and closure of West Marina Station. The station was modernized in 1968, with fluorescent lighting replacing the original gas fixtures. Old platform awnings were demolished and the down-side buildings cleared. Although new canopies were provided, the demolished buildings were not replaced. In July 1969, the unusual tunnel entrance was restored, and it now clearly shows the unusual 'double dentil' arch with tooth decoration.

OPEN-AIR SWIMMING POOL

IN 1927, A campaign started in Hastings and St Leonards for a new outdoor pool. It was spearheaded by the *Hastings Observer*. A scheme was finally approved in 1931 and Sydney Little, the Borough Engineer, was commissioned to do the building. He was well-versed in modern building techniques and chose to build the complex in reinforced concrete. The pool was an Olympic size 330ft by 90ft, nearly as big as Blackpool's. From the air, the design resembled a Greek or Roman amphitheatre, with curved, stepped terracing for spectators on one side and a curved deck for sunbathing on the other. There was an impressive array of diving boards up to 10 metres high, constructed from blocks of concrete. The pool was opened to the public in June 1933. The structure also featured a car park beneath the main seating banks, something that was new to

this type of building in that era. In spite of the pool's many contemporary features, and the bold statement it made about the town, commercially it was not a success. Hastings was desperate to attract visitors. The pool was really much too big for the town to support and there were not enough visitor numbers to achieve the expected results. The Black Rock Pool in Brighton, built around the same time, was only half the size. Hastings' pool only made a profit in its first year of opening. Due to its proximity to the shore, bathers had the option of swimming in the sea, and there were beach huts provided for this purpose. Some of the huts in this area had two levels and, unusually, running water and electricity. As early as 1946, the town council tried to find someone to take up a lease on the pool. Eventually it was turned into the Swimming Pool Holiday Camp by the new owner, Dennis Carrington. There was to be table-tennis, squash and all manner of exciting things to do. Toward the end of the 1970s the property was sold again and renamed the Hastings Holiday Centre, with chalet accommodation for 300 people. However, by now the home holiday market was diminishing, and the complex was closed to the public in 1986. Within a couple of years, and despite some opposition, the complex was demolished. In 1988, efforts were made to save the remaining holiday chalets built around the same time, and there was a proposal to take the matter to a listing appeal. The council, however, demolished them before this could be done. Now the site remains an empty, grassy field awaiting a new future.

YELTON HOTEL

THIS AREA OF Hastings originally had a large chalk headland and this gave its name to the area. The White Rock headland was removed during 1834-1835, allowing the building of a road to connect Hastings and St Leonards, and this opened up new building land along the front between them. The structure of the Yelton Hotel was originally a line of fine late Georgian houses, built around the 1830s. It is believed that the Chalmsford family owned the original buildings and that most of them were used as lodgings for wealthy visitors. In 1887, a Mr and Mrs F. Notley bought the premises with the aim of creating a hotel. The hotel name is the family name reversed. During the 1930s the hotel was modernized with modern toilet and washroom facilities. There have been several owners over the years, and various refurbishment programmes. In 1972 a major fire occurred, and although the hotel was rebuilt, there are now considerably fewer bedrooms than when it first opened. The hotel is now called the White Rock and has recently been refurbished. The picture on the left is from the pre-1901 period, as this was when the hospital next door was sold to be demolished and developed as the new White Rock Theatre.

ROCK-A-NORE ROAD

ALONG THIS ROAD are the net huts: although these are said to be unique to Hastings, some of a similar variety can be found in Whitby. The huts are constructed of weatherboard, with a tarred finish, in an assortment of shapes and sizes. These structures, with a narrow base, were designed to avoid the land tax which was prevalent at the time of their first construction. It is an urban legend that these huts were used for the drying of nets: they only provided storage, whilst the nets were laid out to dry on local common land (known as a 'minis'). The only free fresh-water supply in the Old Town was provided by the East Well Spring, which was completed in March 1849. It was funded from a surplus of donations for rebuilding the net shops following the January 1846 fire, which damaged many of the buildings. A ship, en route from Newcastle to Falmouth, was wrecked

in the gale of October 1857, when it was thrown on the rocks at Rock-a-Nore. Many people tried to rescue the four crewmen, but the sea was too rough and the gale too strong. After an hour, the four men drowned, in front of a large crowd of horrified onlookers. This tragedy set in motion the acquiring of a lifeboat. A local branch of the Royal Humane Society was set up later that month and discussions were held with Hastings Council and the RNLI. A local branch was formed, and its committee met for the first time on 29 January 1858. The lifeboat *Victoria* arrived on Easter Monday, 5 April 1858, and it moved into the lifeboat house which had been built at Rock-a-Nore.

The Corporation of Hastings granted the site of the old Custom House in East Parade, opposite the Lower Lighthouse, for the construction of the new lifeboat house. Charles Arkcoll Jnr paid for the building and boat in memory of his father; it cost £650. Until then, the lifeboat house was at the east end of Rock-a-Nore Road. The new and imposing stone building, shown here on the left, had a tower with a light in. This was to replace the Lower Light, which was being obscured by developments and changes to the shoreline. The old lifeboat house, opposite the Cutter pub, was demolished in December 1959.

Toward the end of the century, harbour works forced the fishermen to move their boats further along the shore. This was to cause controversy, as it was one of the few free places to bathe in the town and was now made perilous by the boats and nets. Although the net huts still exist, the yards (and a nearby drill hall, once used to train local volunteers to repel a feared French invasion) have gone, to be replaced with a Sea Life Centre, museum and toilets.

Other titles published by The History Press

Haunted Hastings

TINA LAKIN

From heart-stopping accounts of apparitions, manifestations and related supernatural phenomena to first-hand encounters with spirits, this collection of stories contains new and well-known spooky tales from in and around Hastings. From the haunted staircase at Hastings library in Claremont and the singing spectre of Hastings College and the phantom coach and horses that gallops up the High Street on a dark winter's night, this phenomenal gathering of ghostly goings-on is bound to captivate anyone interested in the supernatural history of the area

978 0 7524 3827 6

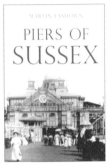

Piers of Sussex

MARTIN EASDOWN

Sussex has a good claim to be the birthplace of the seaside pleasure pier, for although Ryde Pier on the Isle of Wight has the earliest origins as a pier, the famous Chain Pier at Brighton was the first to be used as a fashionable promenade. There followed a rich succession of piers, as they were constructed in Brighton West, Worthing, Bognor, Hastings and Eastbourne. In their heyday they were the place to be seen. Brighton even boasted a 'moving pier', the extraordinary Electric Railway, affectionately known as the 'Daddy-long-legs'. This fascinating volume will explore them all.

978 0 7524 4884 8

Hastings Revisited

ANTHONY KING

This pictorial history traces some of the developments that have taken place in the fishing community of Hastings from the late nineteenth century up to the Second World War. Illustrated with over 200 pictures, mostly drawn from the archives of Hastings Central Library, this volume highlights some of the important events that have occurred in the town.

978 0 7524 3543 5

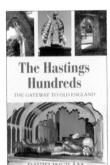

The Hastings Hundreds: The Gateway to Old England

DAVID INGRAM

The Hastings area is famous for the battles that were fought there and most visitors tread the well-worn tourist paths, probably not realising the wealth of history they are missing. Each chapter covers a local area that can be explored on its own or with its neighbours. *The Hasting Hundreds* tells the story of each of the areas, giving details of what there is to see and do. It will hold great appeal for all interested in the history of Hastings.

978 0 7524 4539 7

Visit our website and discover thousands of other History Press books.

www.thehistorypress.co.uk